Finding Myself with *Jesus*

A Poetic Journey from Addiction to Redemption

PAUL MOWERY

ISBN 979-8-89043-901-7 (paperback)
ISBN 979-8-89043-902-4 (digital)

Christian Faith Publishing
832 Park Avenue
Meadville, PA 16335
www.christianfaithpublishing.com

Printed in the United States of America

My (Last) Addiction

Before I started my (last) addiction, I was a financial services representative for MetLife, licensed by the State of Arkansas for life and health insurance. I also carried a series 6 and 63 license with the United States Securities Exchange Commission. I was a charter member and president of the Lake Hamilton Alumni Association and a member at the Hot Springs Chamber of Commerce. As president of its education committee, I was the master of ceremonies for a banquet honoring the top 5% of graduating seniors in Garland County. I was also on a local judges junior advisory board, helping juveniles and their parents with their first offenses.

The end of my second marriage sent me down a rabbit hole. I gave up, lost my spirit, and didn't care what happened to me. The world grazed on me for several years, chipping away at everything I had gained my entire life. I didn't care. I retreated to my bedroom and let the world take over everything past that door.

I met my third wife two years into my last addiction. We tried to battle our tendencies but lost after five years. The devil had strongholds on both of us; we never really had a chance. That failure plunged me into a rabbit hole inside the rabbit hole…

I lost everything I had left in the next two years—myself, material things, and what family I had. Not my proudest moments watching my nephew, a Garland County sheriff, raid my house not once, not twice, but three times. I can't blame them for letting go of what I had become.

Addiction can grab anyone and hold on to you until there is nothing left. You can't get your possessions back, but I am proof that through God, you can get your heart and soul back. God will restore everything you need to become a successful servant with life abundant. All glory goes to God!

If you are struggling with anything, I hope you know that God is waiting for you to ask for help with your heart for He is wanting to help you.

When you are ready for help, although a thirty-day program will change your habits, the longer you stay in a refuge and really work on yourself, the better your chances are at changing your lifestyle and ultimately bettering your life ahead.

Road to Shalom

Due to my addiction, I received my first failure to appear in 2017, resulting in my first arrest at the age of fifty-three and loss of my driver's license. Around this time, although in a family LLC partnership, they cut off my funding. It was their way of helping me. All this put me further at the mercy of the chaos that surrounded me. A little over a month after I had been cut off, I was in a horrible motorcycle accident that I have a very powerful testimony about. Praise the Lord!

When I got home after about a month in the hospital, I was completely abandoned by everyone. I refused to use a wheelchair and was confined to my bedroom. I used a walker to drag myself to the bathroom. I drank water out of the sink. My only visitors were the nurses that would check on me a couple times a week. Broken up, cut off, and abandoned, I found rock bottom. Through the next two months, I had advanced to wearing a back brace and walking with a cane. Only by the grace of God!

I received two more failures to appear after my motorcycle wreck due to my lack of mobility and communication. As soon as I was strong enough and with no other choice, I turned myself in. Judges do not like being disrespected, especially when you don't show up on your court date; rightfully so, they had to be there. My three strikes with the same judge got me his full attention, which in turn landed me in a nine-month, faith-based, recovery program. Thank you, Judge Ralph Ohm. You set me on the right path.

Prayer Request

Addiction has victims on four sides. Good people lose themselves to a power much greater than they expected, ultimately hurting everyone that cares for them, including their animals. I didn't realize that while I was giving up and losing my spirit, God, my family, friends, and dog were hurting with me and because of me.

Fortunately, God is in the restoration business. When you pray through your heart, He hears every word. When you pray, be ready for answers in God's time and in God's understanding.

Pray often, pray for those around you, pray for someone you don't even know, and don't forget to humbly pray for yourself. Always start a prayer with thanks and praise and end it in Jesus's name. Please stop what you are doing right now and pray for something specifically that is on your heart, raise it up to God and let it go.

My prayer is that you start a new daily line of communication with the Lord through prayer. Check out "Pray" page 67.

My Testimony

It was a Sunday morning in October 15, 2017. My income had completely stopped for about a month, and I had not been high in a couple weeks. I was taking notice that I was beating my addiction. I also realized that it had been so long that I forgot how to live straight. Fighting for my life, I spoke these words out loud using my whole heart, "God, Your will be mine if You will give me a place to start and a direction to go in because I have forgotten how to live right."

Be careful of what you ask for. I cringed as soon as I heard the words come out of my mouth. God always has your best interest, and He is not against hard love.

Just hours later that afternoon, I was on my motorcycle in the middle of a curve, and the report states a gust of wind. It sure felt like a big, gentle hand pushed me off the road. It was a violent wreck as I went airborne doing forty-five miles per hour, with a ten-foot drop. I slammed into a washout, flipped over the bike, and went sliding through the woods. As I was sliding to a stop, reaching for my phone to call 911, I knew I was hurt. I remember thinking, "Okay, God, I asked for this, and I know you got me." An overwhelming peace came over me at that very moment. I still have that peace today.

We witness miracles every day, and it is my humble honor to share God's grace in my life with you. I want you to know it is there for the giving if you ask for it through your heart.

Are you ready? My friend made it over to me and asked me to feel her hand; it felt cold. Yes, I had a passenger when I wrecked. Knowing that God was present, I grabbed her hand with both of mine and asked, "Do you believe?"

She said, "Yes."

I then said these words again out loud, "Jesus, use me as a vessel to take her injuries for she is innocent and not a part of what I asked for this morning."

I'm pretty sure she felt His presence because all of a sudden, she pulled her hand away and gave me a look.

It had been close to an hour by the time the ambulance was ready to load us up and take us to the hospital. Two paramedics were looking her over on the embankment by the road. I heard her say that she was okay and didn't need to go to the hospital. I asked her to please go and at least get checked out just in case. She assured me she was okay and not hurting anymore. She was a strong-willed girl that had refused to wear a helmet. The only injury the paramedics could find was a small cut on her forehead at the hairline. They put a Band-Aid on it. That was the only mark on her body after leaving the roadway, airborne, doing forty-five miles an hour. What happened was so profound we only spoke about it once, and she claimed she was sore for a couple days, and that was all. God is real. He hears everything we say and think, and His grace has no boundaries.

Again, are you ready? I had a helmet on, and it was knocked off my head. I broke my jaw and busted a few teeth. I had broken my pelvis, my tailbone in three places, my back in five places, and three ribs. Of the five vertebrae that were broken, the one in the middle was shattered. I was in surgery for four and a half hours while they picked splinters out of my spine. There is only 30 percent of that vertebra left, with hardware holding me upright. For the next six weeks, no one in the hospital would answer me when I asked them if I would be able to walk again. The peace and calmness I received the day of the wreck never left me. By the grace of God, I slowly began to start walking again with the use of a walker.

I am writing this testimony the evening of April 21, 2018, six months and six days after my accident. One more time, are you ready! I don't wear a back brace. I get around pretty good with no help. I am pain free, and I played eighteen holes of golf earlier today. Life is good with God, and it's beyond comprehension.

In closing, I witnessed several miracles that day and was part of two of them. I am humbled and so blessed to have been touched by God's power and grace in my life.

Flash Cards for Living

I was going to provide the flash cards I made to help me change my thought process. Since we are all different, I'm going to give you a simple outline of how to make your own. I believe when we put the work in and create them with God's help, they become exactly what we need.

This is important—pray before you begin. Pray for God to guide you to find the tools you need to help and heal your injured thought process. Pray every time until you complete your flash cards.

First, you need to make a list of emotions where your automatic thought process needs to be changed. Next, title a flash card with each emotion. Now, take your time to write a prayer asking God to help you with a struggle you're having for each emotion. Of course, make sure you ask for it in Jesus's name. This is your first and best line of offense.

Now, it's time to reach in the Bible and pull your specific tools to overcome harmful reactions to your emotions. I used a devotional Bible for men. It had a subject index that sent you to specific verses and readings dealing with each emotion. Make sure you pray for understanding and guidance to help you find your go-to verses. Use up to four verses for quick reference with each emotion.

You're ready. Carry them and use them. Check this out. The more you use them, the lesser you will need them. It is that easy. I hope you try it.

Here is a small list of emotions and feelings. I'm sure you don't need help in all of these areas. Start with just a few you want to change the most. Keep yourself from becoming overwhelmed with how much to work on.

Angry	Frightened	Sad	Suspicious
Mischievous	Disgusted	Turned On	Agonized
Overwhelmed	Perplexed	Guilty	Lonely
Determined	Depressed	Hurt	Withdrawn
Anxious	Miserable	Shocked	Arrogant
Negative	Frustrated	Exhausted	
Ashamed	Regretful	Jealous	

How It All Began

One night early in recovery, I had gone to bed, but I couldn't turn off my mind. I was thinking about a sermon we attended earlier that evening. The words were flowing in my mind so strong that I felt the need to write them down. That night, I wrote "The Road Back to You."

That was the spark which inspired this book. I hope somewhere within the words I have been blessed to write, you will be inspired to become more than your current self.

Without Jesus in my heart and my willful surrender to God, this book would not have been possible. I documented the date and time I started each poem and completed each one within an average of thirty minutes. I am saying this so as you read the words I wrote, you will believe they were assembled by God for you.

I didn't understand at the time, but I kept documenting each one. I wrote forty-four poems in seventy days. I have added several more over the last few years. My hope is at least one is for you. May God bless you, in Jesus's name. Amen!

The Road Back to You

March 24, 2018, 9:00 p.m.

There are many roads and many *yous*. The most important *you* in our lives is God. Through Him, the most difficult of paths become clear, straight, and paved. The next destination is the *you* that you are supposed to be in God's grace. Let's not forget the *yous* in your life that love you and you love as well. Nobody is perfect, and no matter how far we have fallen, when we surrender everything to God through Jesus, He will bless you with everything you need to even rebuild bridges, if need be, and to find the *yous* you need in your life to live happily in God's grace.

Choice

March 25, 2018, 11:00 p.m.

Our number one weapon against adversity is our ability of choice. It is a choice to forgive. It is a choice to move forward. It is a choice to walk in the light of God's grace. It is even a choice to be confident. Ultimately, your life is how you choose it to be. So choose to forgive your past and use that wisdom to choose to stop adversity from entering your future with God.

March 27, 2018, 10:00 p.m.

Father God, please grace those who love me, those I love, and myself with protection from evil forces while I work on myself getting back to your glory. Father God, I pray for this for everyone around me in Jesus's name. Amen.

Are You Ready Now?

March 31, 2018, 10:45 p.m.

God has the only right to judge, and judge He will, every one of us. Although our sins have been paid for through Jesus, we must forgive with love—even ourselves—and actively live within His word to gain His glory and grace for eternity. So don't judge and forgive quickly. Love like you've never been hurt, and know without a doubt, God has the last word.

Don't Just

April 1, 2018, 1:30 p.m.

Don't just pray, get on your knees
Don't just go to church, be an active member
Don't just forgive, raise it up, and move forward
Don't just love, love unconditionally
Don't just think, speak it out loud, and hear what you say
Don't just fall, get back up, and keep fighting
Don't just be yourself, become more than yourself
Don't just believe, have faith
Don't just, just do

Rehab Revelation, God's Newest Army

April 2, 2018, 9:30 p.m.

You are not alone, you are everywhere
You are not crazy, you have been prepared
You are not broken, you have been built back
You are not simple, you are sharp as a tack
Let's walk in the word, it's time to help our fallen
Witness and testify, this is your callin'
God is waiting for us to give Him His due
And retake this world for me and you

Awaken and Rise

April 3, 2018, 9:30 p.m.

Why are you still waiting? What is your hesitation?
God will clear the path for your destination
He will strike fear and hate from your senses
You will be set free, no more fences
Wake up, wake up, wake up, wake up, wake up, wake up, wake up
Now that you are awake, I dare you to rise up and get in the fight
Get in the word, walk in the light, do what's right
The more you do, the easier life will be
Stop thinking about it, live it, and you will see
God is ready to help you
So wake up, rise up, and do

The Shower Cleansing

April 5, 2018, 8:00 a.m.

Our bodies get dirty, we shower to keep them clean
We do it often, trying to keep our bodies pristine
As we clean the outside, we often think about the inside
Eight out of ten times, it is usually something dealing with our pride
Ain't no better time to focus on ourselves
Walk in that closet, and clean off those shelves
Release your past, forgive your sin
And let God wash it away like the dirt on your skin

It's Time to Sink This "Boat"

April 5, 2018, 5:00 p.m.

Cancer is a fungus with a high death rate
Ice is also, so why are you serving it on that plate?
It's time to pick which side you are on
It's really easy, don't you want your stuff back out of pawn?
It's not about whatever floats your boat
You can be forgiven if you have already wrote that note
Pray to God to help you change your ways
Pray from your heart, and watch what happens within the next few days
When you're blown away by His response to your prayer
It's time, to step up, don't turn away, don't you dare
He will help you regain your strength
It's time for this "*boat*" to sink

One at a Time

April 5, 2018, 11:00 p.m.

It is time to lock the doors and keep everyone back
It is time to separate yourself from the pack
Do it now before it's too late
Do it before you lose your love to hate
They don't love you, they never did
They will bleed you till you are dead
Start reading the Word, walking in the light
Everything you have been through will disappear without a fight
God will heal you, rebuild your temple
Pray, believe, and have faith, it's that simple
He will bless your commitment with His grace
Guaranteed to restore the smile on your face

Energy Spent

April 6, 2018, 8:30 p.m.

Look at the time and energy you spend bringing yourself down
Turn it around
Get back on your feet
Don't stop till your complete
Pray for steps to be shone
Do it right and God will set them in stone
Don't just hear what I'm saying
Get on your knees and start praying
Start spending that energy on good instead of bad
Start living the life you are supposed to have

Just for Today

April 13, 2018, 1:00 a.m.

Just for today, I want to see
If I can be who God wants me to be
I'm going to be strong and true
I'm going to choose the right thing to do
Just for today, I'm going to live, laugh, and love
I'm going to change my stars above
This is *just* the start
This is *for* my heart
Just for *today*

Me, Myself, and God

April 14, 2018, 8:40 a.m.

You're not special, you're a unique person
Everyone is just like you but a different version
In order to get it right, we need to unite
Get in the Word, and start walking in the light
Stop being self-centered, start helping each other
In God's eyes, that's your brother
You are unique and powerful, yearn for it
Harness it right or you will burn for it
Pray for it, get in the Word and read
God will help you with everything you need
Time to rewind and be all you can be
Start hustling for God not just for myself and me

Into the Refuge

April 16, 2018, 5:00 p.m.

Everywhere you look, there ain't no place to hide
One day, you are going to wake up and find out you died
Into the refuge is where you need to go
God is there waiting for you to show
Be at ease now, know that you are protected
Work on yourself, pray for it, and your spirit can be resurrected
It's easy to focus on what you can't do
Step up to the plate, and focus on you
Read the Word, have faith in the light
It won't be easy; the devil will put up a fight
That's why into the refuge is where you need to be
God will grace you there, do it and you will see

Think Before You Happen

April 16, 2018, 11:00 p.m.

Think before you say or do
Give yourself some time to get a clue
Impulse is not our best side
It can take us on a heck of a ride
Every time you think before you happen
You change your course, you are the captain
Pray for the steps to be taken
And God will help you see the ones to be makin'
Open your heart, and let Jesus in
He is ready to help you win
So treat as you would like to be treated
It's time to stop being conceited

The Anger Train

April 18, 2018, 8:00 a.m.

Almost instantly, when something goes wrong
The back of my mind starts playing that song
I hear that train is coming, coming around the bend
God show me how to stop that train, it's got to end
That anger train is loaded, full of all my hurt
I'm praying Jesus will help me derail it, put it in the dirt
I need to change my way of thinking, start praying to
This is not the easy way, it's the right thing to do
I'm going to focus on being kind
Erase the anger train from my mind
If I ask Him, God will have my back
As long as I'm trying, He will step in when I lack
The battle is real, but don't fear
With God on your side, the tracks will clear

He Will

April 20, 2018, 5:30 a.m.

Open your mind and your heart to let God in
He will not hurt you
He will not desert you
He will help you mend
He will stay with you till the end
He will answer your prayers
He will show you He cares
He will comfort you in the storm
He will guide you back if you roam
He will provide everything you need
Live, pray, love, hope, believe, have faith, and read

Chance Change

April 20, 2018, 9:30 a.m.

Change is not easy at all
It creates a chance to fall
If you change and let Jesus in
Chances are you will defeat sin
Change from bad to good will challenge you
Take a chance with God, and experience what He can do
The more you change, the easier it will be
The more chances you take, the more you will see
As you change, watch yourself grow
Chances are, you already know
What are you waiting for
Take some chances to change
And change your chances in life

Beating the Odds

April 21, 2018, 6:40 p.m.

Limitless events can spark the start of an addiction
But across the board, we all suffer the same affliction
Plain and simple, we stop dreaming and give up on our goals
And start digging ourselves some very deep holes
Although we are aware of what is happening to us
The harder we try, the worse it gets when we put up a fuss
When you are ready to save yourself, God can help you on your way
Open your heart, let Jesus in it, start praying today
You must forgive, even yourself, for everything that went bad
Put your past behind you, quit grieving about what you had
Surround yourself with people that love you, love yourself to
The world is ready for you to get back to you

God Cannot Hurt You

April 22, 2018, 6:00 p.m.

God does not possess the ability to hurt us
Jesus guaranteed that, He is driving the bus
We have all been hurt before
Some of us so deep it shattered our core
I understand shutting down, faking it, letting no one in
Did you know that in God's eyes you are committing a sin?
You are hurting yourself, giving no love to yourself too
You have to use your heart, or it will be the death of you
God has never hurt anyone, He will love you at the drop of a dime
His love has never faltered, standing the test of time

I know you are scared to let Jesus in your heart
I was also at the start
But when I surrendered myself completely to Him
We forgave me, I no longer carried my sin
When you love God, He will love you back
He will show off for you, that's a fact
God is not like everyone else that made you hurt
He wants to spend eternity with you and will always help you up out
of the dirt

The Devil in Disguise

April 24, 2018, 9:15 a.m.

The closer we get to God, the harder the devil will try
He can manipulate those close to you to look you in the eye and lie
He will use whoever he can to get to you
God will help you, this is what to do
Forgive them quickly, do it with your heart
The devil is in the battle as long as we stay apart
Pray for them to rid the devil from their life
Hope for them to start walking in the light
For it is not them, it's the devil's goal
They are just like you, and the devil also wants their soul
We have got to pull together, in numbers we are strong
Let's expose the devil for what he is, and that is he is wrong

Walking on Water

April 25, 2018, 7:15 a.m.

Jesus did it, Peter did too
Have faith, walk the walk, and so can you
Walking on water today is a metaphor
For letting Jesus in your heart and changing your core
Believe, have faith, and pray
Don't just let Him in, help Him stay
Walk the walk, and talk the talk
In no time, your faith will be solid as a rock
So walk on that water for everyone to see
Accept Jesus in your heart and be all you can be

The Bad Seed

April 25, 2018, 6:15 p.m.

How can you believe in your own lies?
You will stay in denial, even if somebody dies
Sad thing is the one pointing you out
Is just like you, without a doubt
It's the new way to be
It's what you tell them, not what they see
You might get away with it for now
When you stand before God, you're going to have a cow
Keep telling yourself you're not doing wrong
When it's time for eternity, you're going to get the gong

My Attention

April 27, 2018

It used to be a bad thing to gain
If you did, I brought the thunder and rain
More than likely, you had it coming
And the storm got worse if you tried running
Now, Jesus is in my heart
Giving my attention a brand new start
As hate fades away, love is moving in
Every day, it gets easier not to sin
Now, when you get my attention, this is what you will see
The man in front of you, with love in his heart, is me

Not a Chance

April 28, 2018, 11:00 a.m.

If you are not there, they can't blame you
There is not a chance to guess at what you do
Avoid the entire situation
Do it without hesitation
People jump to think you will do wrong
The rumors spread, and you are labeled bad before long
It's best to stop it before it starts
Don't put yourself where someone can hurt you with remarks
Every time you are alone with someone
A rumor can escalate into you being hung
So keep perspectives from the ability to enhance
Don't be there, then there is not a chance

Right and Wrong

April 28, 2018, 11:35

Some people tend to obey
Some people are more likely to stray
The ones that obey are easy to teach
The ones that stray are hard to reach
When you find God and submit, it becomes natural to do right
If you want God but won't commit, you wander between dark and light
Here is some wisdom from how I am living
It is your soul, and it is to God you should be giving
So quit straying and putting up a fight
At the end of the day, you will sleep better at night

Beholding Beauty

April 29, 2018, 9:15 p.m.

Beauty is in the eye of the beholder
It doesn't matter how you look or what's in your folder
Although you may have good assets
A beholder is looking for your lack of regrets
The best way to achieve this goal
Is to surrender to God, promise Him your soul
For you achieve divine beauty walking in the light
It is truly a heavenly sight
When love is what you give, love will be what you get
The beholder is a lover, and through God, you will be set

Standing Ground

May 1, 2018, 8:00 a.m.

It's easy to remove yourself from a situation
Sometimes, it's a reflex and done without hesitation
If you step away from everything, that is a little abrasive
You lose out on a chance to grow and be creative
Pray about it, and stand your ground more
When you are doing what is right, let them here you roar
The more you gain, the brighter you will shine
With Jesus in your heart, you are right on time
So stand your ground, be proud of who you are
In life you, will go far

If I Died Today

May 2, 2018, 8:45 p.m.

Have I told you that I love you?
Have I done all that I can do?
Will you remember me?
Did I help you is the key
Know I have Jesus in my heart
In the end, that's a good start
Be happy for me, keep a smile on your face
I'm going to be in a better place
I want to leave you with this
Get right with God, heaven, you don't want to miss

People Hurting Hurt People

May 2, 2018, 8:45 p.m.

When you have been hurt and it scarred your heart
You need to forgive or you will start
Hate will begin to build inside of you
You will start hurting others, it's what we do
It might be physical or using your voice
Words are just as damaging as stones, only by choice
Pray for God to help with your pain
The more you use your heart, the more you will gain
Love and forgive yourself, first of all
Then forgive those that hurt you for dropping the ball
Break the chain of hurt in your life
Tell the devil to go fly a kite

Growing Back

May 6, 2018, 10:50 p.m.

You have been cut down
I'm talking all the way to the ground
Don't waste your time on what used to be
Close your past quickly, set yourself free
Pray, laugh, and open your heart
Having a vision is a really good start
As you start to grow back
Ask God to help you when you lack
In no time, you will be reaching for the sky
This time, don't drop the ball, you know why

God's Time

May 10, 2018, 4:00 p.m.

Time is a figment of our imagination
It becomes eternal when we reach our destination
When we wish it away or wait, it can stand still
It passes so fast when we look back, was it real?
With Jesus in your heart and God on your side
Time doesn't matter, just enjoy the ride
If you have strayed and want Him back
You have to work for it, that's a fact
Plant your seeds, don't wish or wait
Before you know it, in God's time, you will be standing at the gate

Free Yourself

May 12, 2018, 5:20 p.m.

Do you like being down?
Stuck in a rut, not gaining ground
Would you like some help to win that fight?
There is only one answer that is right
Pray about it, let Jesus in your heart
Ask for forgiveness from God, that's a start
Don't forget to forgive yourself too
Then forgive those that have hurt you
If you can do it with real love
That weight holding you down will be lifted from above

Collateral Damage

May 14, 2018, 7:50 a.m.

You affect everyone around you
With everything you say or do
When you speak or act in a negative way
It is possible for you to ruin someone's day
Stop your negativity and hate
Do it now before it's too late
Go to church, read the Bible, that's a good start
To rid the hurt and hate from your heart
Forgive those that caused you to hate
Do you want their sins to be your fate?
You have the ability to show people right from wrong
Choose to live right, it will become your nature before long

Staying True

May 14, 2018, 8:00 p.m.

Now you got Him, it is up to you to keep Him there
Praise Him, work your heart, show you care
If you fall, be quick to rise
Praise God that you're alive
Pray as often as you can
You will shine being a good man
Lead by example, this is your calling
Be quick to witness if you see someone falling
There is so much glory in staying true
How empowering to see the man in the mirror is you

In the End, It Begins

May 16, 2018

Success in life is measured by how we weathered the storm
The battle of good and evil can leave us worn out and torn
We all fight this battle throughout our life
In the end, it matters that our heart is right
Grace is given, and battles are won
With God on your side, you never have to run
Pray for God to show you the way, to let you see
With Him is where you want to be
Surrender to Him so in the end
You will be in the right place for eternity to begin

Why Are You Here

May 18, 2018

We forget to look at the big picture nowadays
Try thinking about others and not just getting your way
Respect others if you want to reach your goals
You will get nowhere with your character full of holes
You have to give it to get it
And I'm not talking about sarcastic wit
I'm saying compassion and love for a start
You have one, try using your heart
If you're not willing to help your brother battle his fear
My question to you is, why are you here?

Tend Your Garden

May 21, 2018, 9:00 p.m.

When you find that you have hardened your heart
Ask God to help you regrow it, a fresh start
You have to change your ways like you till a garden
That means you must give yourself a full pardon
Then you need to forgive those that helped you get that way
Giving yourself fertile soil at the end of the day
Now plant your seeds by doing what's right
Water your needs, keep growing in the light
Stop the growth of weeds, it must be tended
Before you know it, your heart will be mended

Bending Your Own End

May 23, 2018, 9:00 a.m.

Rules are not made to be broken
When it comes to God, ain't no joking
With earthly rules, you flirt with disaster
With God's rules, you're changing your ever after
Bend 'em or break 'em, it ends the same way
You crossed the line at the end of the day
You might get away with it while you are walking the earth
In the end, you answer for everything you did since birth
So be careful about how many rules you break or bend
You are changing how you will be dealt with in the end

Pull Your Weight

May 23, 2018, 6:30 p.m.

You got yourself in this
What part of that did you miss?
Stop pointing that finger away from you
Start taking responsibility for everything you do
Not just the stuff that makes you look good
I'm talking about all the shady stuff, you should
We are all in this together
You are not light as a feather
Start changing your fate
By pulling your weight

It Takes You

May 24, 2018, 9:00 a.m.

Time for you to step up to the plate
Break a sweat, change your fate
No one can do this for you
So get a grip, catch the clue
Open your mind for a start
Now let's dust off your heart
Pray for God to help you every day
You must do the work then He will show you the way
Only you can do it to get it right
Roll up your sleeves, you're in for a fight
It's not simple to change yourself from wrong to right
You will be glad you did at the end of the night
Choose wisely, the way you live
It is easy to take, but better to give

The Struggle Is Real

May 27, 2018, 10:00 a.m.

Everyday life ain't what it used to be
Now add the perspectives of how people see
The world is complex, with so many angles
There is so much more that bad people dangle
The innocent can so quickly become bad
It's too late when you realize you have been had
Just when you think you have reached the end
That's when the real struggle begins
It's not easy to break the chains of addiction
The chance you will not is most people's predictions
To win the battle, you need God on your side
When you surrender to Him, you're in for a ride
Refilling your heart with love is the deal
Don't give up, these days, the struggle is real

Right Now

May 27, 2018, 8:00 p.m.

Right now, God is with you
He knows everything you think, say, and do
Right now, He loves you with all His might
Respect and love Him back and for you He will fight
Right now, surrender to Him if you have not
If you don't, I hope you like it hot
Right now, forgive everyone and yourself too
Then pray through Jesus to save you
Right now, before time gets away
And you don't have another day

No Offense

May 28, 2018, 6:30 p.m.

It is dangerous when you become offended
It can hurt you even if it was not intended
When you get upset about what other people do
If you are not careful, it can really affect you
They don't care if you get upset
Chances are they're self-centered, you can bet
The best thing you can do is pray for them
And hope you don't have to deal with it again
You must forgive their offense and let it go
Before it turns to hate, just say no

Love = Time

June 1, 2018, 7:30 a.m.

Love someone for a moment, and the moment is gone
That's not love, you are wrong
Only love can stand the test of time
Love fills your soul, heart, and mind
When you're in love, time stands still
Because you never get your fill
God's love is so pure it spawned eternity
He wants us to join Him for this journey
This is true, no trick, or witty rhyme
Love = time

The Best Stuff

June 4, 2018, 8:15 a.m.

Now that my thoughts are right and my ways are good
My life is getting back in order as it should
I have come so far in such a short time
God is helping with my heart while I work on my mind
Staying in the light and reading the Word are my new addictions
With Jesus in my heart, I will beat my afflictions
I have forgiven myself; I love myself too
I am smiling again, that, I almost forgot how to do
I hope you are saved and living this way
If you are not or you are trying, for you I will pray
Please get to know God for if you do not
Hell is real, and that's where you were rot
I'm not just being mean, I care for you, I'm just saying
If you want to be in heaven with me, you better start praying

It's This Simple

June 4, 2018

When I keep my emotions suppressed
Before long, I become depressed
I'm quick to medicate this affliction
That soon turns into an addiction
That's how a suppressed affliction
Becomes a depressed addiction

Real Talk

June 7, 2018, 8:30 a.m.

Life isn't how you make it, it's what you make of it
It's not measured by how much you get
It is about the struggles you face the day you start to crawl
How you deal with adversity every time you fall
Integrity is what it's all about
Who you are when no one is looking, without a doubt
Heaven is our goal to get in
To get there, you must battle sin
In today's world, you're in for a constant fight
You will need rest, do good so you can sleep at night
Doing things how you want may not be the best way
When you find yourself struggling, get on your knees and pray
Keep God in your life, don't wheel and deal
And when it comes to talk, keep it real

Help

June 8, 2018, 10:00 a.m.

Don't kick yourself, use that energy to get off the ground
Dust yourself off, and get ready for the next round
You know you don't have to do it all alone
When you pray to Jesus, it's like talking to Him on the phone
As long as you are trying, God is there for you
He will help you in everything you do
Keep reading the Word and living right
He will show you how to win the fight
In His grace is where to stay
For Him to help you every day

Step Up

June 11, 2018 7:00 a.m.

If you are in church and going through the motions
Take the next step, and give God your devotion
Go all in, and at the end of the day
You will see that God is with you every step of the way
Don't take my word for it
Live it, and see what you get
I'm not talking about a single material thing
It's the love, joy, and praise your heart will sing
With Jesus in your heart, it's a whole new life
To keep Him there, step up and live right

Judgment

June 12, 2018, 7:30 a.m.

It's a sin to give it out
Discernment is for us to have no doubt
Judges give it to keep our order
With all due respect to one border
In the end, only God has it to give
And His judgment is based on how we lived
We all have it in us to know bad from good
Don't take the path you want, take the one you should
If you can feel good about everything you do
You will be in the right place when God judges you

Who's to Blame

June 13, 2018, 8:00 a.m.

This is how this happened to me
Listen to what I say, and you will see
It doesn't matter, I was there
I am innocent, it's not fair
Did you know that wrongful pointing of that finger is a sin?
Denial is an argument you only think you win
Until the day you meet your Maker
And you're sentenced a liar and a faker
You know what happened, you really were there
Confess your actions, you need to care
So get out that finger and fix your aim
Remember, God always knows, who's to blame

Plain and Simple

June 17, 2018, 8:30 a.m.

What's so hard to figure out
God is real, there is no doubt
Jesus paid the price for all of our sins
Still, we must surrender and repent to get in
Heaven that is, it is real too
Loved ones you have lost are there waiting for you
So quit putting off what you already know
Till that dirt up, you have seeds to sow
You have people counting on you, here and there
So get your shine on and show you care

Unlocked

June 23, 2018, 6:15 p.m.

You can still love yourself
So take your heart off that shelf
Dust it off, wipe it clean
That way, you will no longer be mean
To repair your heart and let Jesus in
Forgive yourself to erase your sin
Surrender to God, and at the end of the day
He will clear a path and show you the way
Share your love, don't be afraid to live
With God on your side, you will receive more than you give
Take your life back before it's too late
Do it right if you want keys to the gate

Courageous Spirit

June 26, 2018 6:30 a.m.

It isn't a feeling or emotion
It is more like a conviction or devotion
It is used in extreme times, in desperation, and in war
It's not something learned, it's part of your core
We all have it, some more than others
It takes a lot of it when you decide to recover
You use it when you surrender to God above
It is a big part of love
Let's all be a hero today
And use our courage in some way
I promise the more you do
The better life will get for you

The Truth

July 8, 2018, 6:00 p.m.

You know what it is all about
It is what it is, without a doubt
Why is it so elusive?
We are prone to lie and be reclusive
If you told it, you wouldn't be in denial
And have to carry around that big pile
Whether it be right or devastating
God knows it and is waiting
You need to own up and confess your ways
Do it before you run out of days
When you finally step up, you will see
The truth really will set you free

Not Alone

July 12, 2018, 8:00 p.m.

So you're winning against your addictions
Leaving behind your afflictions
Beating the odds and haters' predictions
There will be times that you feel alone
Remember how much you have grown
Now you have God on your side
He's not just along for the ride
Through His grace, you don't have to hide
Find someone from church and talk about it
Do it every time you doubt, don't fret
Soon you will know, you are not alone

Pray

August 10, 2018 9:45 a.m.

Pray for help with a need
Pray to separate and weed
Pray to start each day
Pray for guidance along the way
Pray if you stumble or fall
Pray like He has a phone, give Him a call
Pray and thank Him when times are good
Pray and praise Him in bad times, you should
Pray standing, sitting, or kneeling, it doesn't matter how
Pray, pray now

One Day at a Time

August 27, 2018, 1:15 p.m.

What a blessing, the dawn on a new day
Start with prayer, thanks, and help for the way
Smile while you talk, remember to be kind
Try not to do things you will want to rewind
Move forward, another day to do what's right
Keep that conscience clear so sleep will come easy tonight
If adversity comes your way
Be quick to pray about it, keep it at bay
Stay in the Word, walk in the light
Eternal life is your reward for living right

No Title

Standing in the light
Living right
Along comes the night
Where we must fight
Use His might
And fly like a kite
Keeping your height
Till the dawn of a new day

God's Way

September 10, 2018, 11:00 a.m.

God is ready to teach us with all of His affection
He loves to help us especially if we ask for direction
You must ask for it, that's your best start
And when you do, pray for it through your heart
Choose your words wisely and always end this way
Thank you for listening, Lord, in Jesus's name I pray
When He answers you, whether good, bad, or what you think is
    devastation
Praise Him for His grace without hesitation

Remember, some answered prayers are hard to swallow
Yet every time we look back, it was the right path to follow
So what are you waiting for? Get on your knees and pray
God's ready to show you the way

Thank God

September 12, 2018

I have come so far yet can slip so fast
Trying to keep my future from looking like my past
The struggle never stops, trying every day
I stay focused on God, every second of the way
If the devil tricks me and gets my attention
I'm quick to kneel and heartfully say it wasn't my intention
He forgives me as soon as I forgive myself
How did I survive, trying this without His help?
Thank you for your love, Lord, thank you for your rod
Thank you, thank you, thank you, God

Letting Go

September 17, 2018 7:30 a.m.

If it doesn't work, we don't want it
Don't we all like our clothes to fit?
What's so different between our things and life
Why does it seem so hard to live right?
Something keeps getting in the way
We are stuck in a rut, some people say
Only God can help us out
Steps must be made, ain't no doubt
Throw your old self out, just like your trash
You're broken and don't fit, it isn't rash
You'll feel so much better when you do
Time to let go and trade up to a new you

The Ultimate Gift

October 19, 2018

Let me tell you a little something about this place called Shalom
For nine months, it was my refuge, now I call it home
When I first arrived, I did not want to stay
They said that is normal, at first, everyone feels that way
They were patient with me as I put my past to rest
The sides I showed them were not my best
I'll never forget the day I started my surrender
Choosing to listen, instead of hinder
It was hard to trust again, give Jesus the wheel
But if you want to succeed in life, that's the deal
As I worked on myself, my heart started growing back
They help me stay focused, keeping me on track
Nine months is a really short time
To change your ways that is, it is quite the climb
Now that I have completed this chapter
My journey begins to the ever after
Armed with tools to guard myself and still love with all my heart
Walking in God's grace is so right, the gift of a fresh start
Thank you, Shalom, for everything you have done
And I want you to know, as for me, you won

Believe

October 21, 2018, 6:30 a.m.

Life is not for us to figure out
We only make it difficult with doubt
When we remove ourselves and let Jesus in
Every single time, we will win
Our part in the fight is to have faith and believe
For the more you do, the more you receive
I am saying this from experience I am living
Wisdom formed from trials, I am giving
Be quick to forgive and fast to pray
Walk the walk as best you can in His way
Know each time life tries to take you out

With God, you can triumph anything, ain't no doubt
God is real, I believe in Him
I love Him and no longer desire to sin
My hope is everyone will feel this way
For the Bible says, it all changes forever that day

Prepared

November 2, 2018, 10:45 p.m.

The time has come to apply my learning
To think before I leap at things I am yearning
The devil will try to get me to forget my lessons
When distraught or tempted, I must quickly count my blessings
I will pray every day and stay in my devotions
Using my mind and heart to subdue my emotions
It's a cruel world out there in which we live
I must not borrow offences, be quick to forgive
Now that I am saved, the real battle has begun
Just by following His light, I will have won
I will stay in the Word, be steadfast and true
Paying attention to everything I think, say, and do
I am so glad I have changed my thinking, actions, and ways
Never again will I allow myself to walk around in a daze
I say this with confidence, let me tell you why
Whether now or later, I know I will meet Him when I die

Good Judgment to Judge Ralph Ohm

November 7, 2018, 10:00 a.m.

The eight years before I met you was a continuous spiral down
Once strong, I became lost, thank God I was found
At first, I struggled with your order
Even made plans to run for the border
Where you sent me, helped me with my surrender
Where I first thought you were just mean, you turned out to be my
    defender
I have my heart back with a new start, thanks to you
I wish everyone would take advantage of the things you do
I personally want to thank you for everything you have done
And I want you to know, as for me, you won

Food for Thought

January 21, 2020, 3:45 p.m.

Here's the dill
The world is about to be in a pickle
The end-times are coming, so stop being fickle
Better straighten up, ain't no place to run
The day He arrives, playing on the fence is done
On that day, you're either going to heaven or hell
Heaven is eternal bliss, hell is eternal jail
It's up to you as to where you are going
My advice is to get in that book and get that spirit flowing
Just food for thought, I'll leave you with this
If He comes today, are you burning in hell, or receiving eternal bliss?

Time, Love, and God

February 2, 2021, 12:00 p.m.

When I was young, I had it all figured out.
I was in charge of my destiny; I had no doubt.
I relied on me, to figure out this stuff.
I was saved, and I thought that was enough.
I have tried and failed several times at love.
I got one left in me, and the only place I'm looking is above.
To be honest, on my own, I didn't do so well.
I let the world overtake me, I was living in hell.
I think God created bottom, so while we are still alive, we have to
    look up.
When we take the steps, He reaches down and pulls us out of the
    muck.
From now on, my focus will stay on Him.
Through faith, everything I do will be a win.
The one thing I need is someone by my side.
My faith is strong, and my heart is open wide.
Today's world is changing for the worst, growing wicked and odd.
So I'm not wasting my time looking for love without God.

The Lesser of Two Lessons

February 8, 2021, 3:45 p.m.

Next time you are thinking about the severity of a storm you went through, what if God put you on that path because the one you were headed for was more than you could have handled?

Most blessings are easy to see.
Some are hidden, here is a key.
Storms are no fun.
They usually have us on the run.
When we finally set still and let God in.
The storm subsides to clear skies again.
Usually, we are off our path to God.
And the storm is an extension of His rod.
Correction comes before the end.
And if we listen and obey, we get in.

Heaven that is, if you were wondering.
We don't go there when we are blundering.
God is quick to give us correction.
He does it for our protection.
When the path is more than we can handle.
It really isn't a storm, it's a candle.
So from now on, when you are counting your blessings.
Remember your storms, they were likely the lesser of two lessons.

Get Persistent

October 24, 2021 11:30 a.m.

How did I get here? So down
Like quicksand sinking in the ground
I need help to get out of this mess
I need to reboot, I need some rest
I need to go where I can grow
They will know, how to start the flow
God, help me figure it out

How did I get here? So confused
I've already dealt with my issues
Walking in the light, doing right
I sleep when I go to bed at night
Borrowed offenses getting accumulated
Next thing I know, getting frustrated
God, help me figure it out

We are human, we drop the ball
We are not failures at all
How we react is the key
Persistence will set you free
On your own, it's hard to win
Being alone opens you up to sin
The thing is we need each other
That is why I call you, brother
We need God to help with this transformation
All working together for our salvation

As long as we stay on this path
We will avoid His wrath
So let's get persistent together
And ride out this weather
God, help us figure it out

Praise God for Easter

What a world we live in today
It's not so easy to find one's way
Through life that is, a lot of obstacles
Year by year, growing more diabolical
I have good news for you today
A man named Jesus paved the way
A long time ago, He died for our sin
Giving us salvation, a guaranteed win
He rose from the dead on this day
Leaving no doubt, He is the way
Not just to our destination
Also the guide for our preparation
This journey is easy to start
Let Him into your heart
Read, believe, have faith, and pray
He will even wait for you if you stray
The world is steadily falling the other direction
Accept Jesus in your heart for your salvation
If you do this before it is too late
You will meet Him at the gate
He is the Alpha and Omega, the fixer
Praise God for Easter

Goals

March 8, 2023 3:00 a.m.

This world is full of traps and snares
Evil is real, and it wants your soul
Worldly ways are growing stronger every day
And the one in the wilderness has many ways to achieve this goal
The way to overcome the world was gifted to us long ago
The ultimate sacrifice by Jesus set it in stone
We even have a book that has stood the test of time
An instruction manual on how to make it home
God is the light that can bring you out of the darkness

All you have to do is raise your hand
When you find yourself lost in the wilderness
He will show up and shine when you reach out and make a stand
Praise God for His grace
Jesus protects our soul
The Holy Spirit lives in us
Believe, have faith, and pray to reach His goal
All you have to do is raise your hand
He will show up and shine when you reach out and make a stand

Praise the Lord

There is someone that can lift us when we are confused, hurting, or down
When we can't take it anymore and our chin is on the ground
You don't have to give in to the chaos, corruption, and pain
Open your heart, and praise Him, stand in the spirit, and feel Him reign
Praise the Lord
When the pain is more than you can stand
Praise the Lord
When your life is getting out of hand
Praise the Lord
When you are down in the ground
Praise the Lord
When you are ready to be found
He is waiting for you to call to Him, so use your voice, say it out loud
Lift up your hands, and look up to the clouds
The sky will light up as you feel the joy enter your heart
Your pain will fade, mind will clear, this is where to start
Praise the Lord
Raise up your voice, let Him hear you roar
Praise the Lord
Do this, and you will feel it down to your core
Praise the Lord
Not just on Sunday, do it every day
Praise the Lord
If you stay consistent, the blues will fade away
So praise him, be proud to show the world where you stand
You will soon understand why there was only one set of footprints
    in the sand

Acknowledgments

All glory goes to God! Praise the Lord!

Thank you for your interest in my thoughts as I overcame my addictions and reestablished my relationship with Jesus. God has helped me use what I have put myself through to connect with and encourage others that are trying to break free from addiction. I am still working for Shalom. I am so blessed that I found God's purpose for me. I am surrounded by Christian people who have chosen to work on the front lines, fighting the good fight. My circle is strong, and I love every one of you!

I want to thank everyone that has been in my life. The good, the bad, and the indifferent, without you, I wouldn't be who I am today.

This is a special shout out to my brothers and sisters of Shalom Recovery Centers. I hope every one of you are living a blessed life without the afflictions that brought us together.

It took a village to help me get my spirit back and change my life. Thank you Judge Ralph Ohm, Mrs. Lain Rodgers, Marty and Lisa Haynes, Jackie Walker, Pastor Dave Holland, Pastor Lance Arguello, Pastor Andrew Gonzalez, Pastor Jeff Efird, Fallon, Rachel, Casey, and Terri. I was stubborn and broken when I met you, and your efforts helped me find my purpose. Words can't express my gratitude.

If you are like me and needed help, may I suggest a faith-based recovery program lasting at least six months—long enough to establish a healthy schedule and a new way of life. It takes time to accept and become a new person with a new lifestyle, but it is so worth it.

Every rehab center has their problems; staff is human also. When you go to work on yourself, be careful not to focus on the negativity. Remember, it takes *you* to make it work.

About the Author

His father had a prostate procedure that out of one hundred thousand surgeries, 100 percent of the patients were sterile. A few months after the surgery, his mother became pregnant. I know what you're thinking, but before you go there, when his mother turned sixteen and could date, the only man she went on a date with—the man she married—was his father.

His parents were married for fifty-six years before his father passed away at the age of seventy-five. His mother passed in 2021 at the age of ninety. His sister passed away in early 2001; she was fifteen years older. His brother that many people throughout their lives asked if they were twins; he is ten years older. His mother was thirty-three, and his father was thirty-four when he was born in 1964.

Turns out his father had two sperm tubes. The chances of his being conceived was 0.0001 percent, literally one in a million. He was named after the doctor that performed the surgery. His grandfather, father, brother, and nephew are all named Charlie; he is Paul.

He had a sheltered childhood and was eighteen before he was introduced to the real world. He moved out without his parents' blessing. He lasted about six months. He was having a blast he just didn't take time to eat. It probably had something to do with a large bag of black mollies his friends and he ate like candy.

Back when the meth was real, it cost his first marriage in the fifth year. After being raised the way he was, he considered himself a huge failure. He went buck wild for a few years and became a thrill seeker—if it was dangerous, he was in. Then one day, all of the sudden, something clicked in his head. He quit and walked away from everything he knew, on his own.

He owned and operated a gym for a few years, but his kindness didn't get the bills paid. He met his second wife as he started a career from the bottom up as a brick mason. Fifteen years of hard labor took its toll on his body, so he had to switch to his brains. When his sister passed away from a very quick battle with cancer and having no insurance, he was compelled to understand how and why insurance works. He became a financial services representative for MetLife during the last five years of his second marriage. Due to irreconcilable differences in his second marriage that lasted seventeen years, he turned back to meth.

This book is his account, through poetry, of finding who he is with Jesus in his heart.